★CUBAN
Cocktails

★CUBAN
Cocktails

Over 50 mojitos, daiquiris and
other refreshers from Havana

Katherine Bebo

RYLAND PETERS & SMALL
LONDON • NEW YORK

For my lovely, crazy sister Lizzie. Thanks for lending me your Bacardi bottle – can't believe Dad sold it!

Senior Designer Barbara Zúñiga
Commissioning Editor Stephanie Milner
Picture Manager Christina Borsi
Production Sarah Kulasek-Boyd
Art Director Leslie Harrington
Editorial Director Julia Charles
Publisher Cindy Richards
Indexer Hilary Bird

First published in 2016 by
Ryland Peters & Small
20–21 Jockey's Fields
London WC1R 4BW
and
341 E 116th Street
New York, 10029

www.rylandpeters.com

10 9 8 7 6 5 4 3 2 1

Text © Michael Butt, Ross Dobson, Lydia France, Ben Fordham, Felipe Fuentes Cruz, Carol Hilker, Louise Pickford, Ben Reed, Jennie Shapter, Milli Taylor, Sunil Vijayakar, Fran Warde, Laura Washburn, William Yeoward and Ryland Peters & Small, 2016. See page 128 for details.

Design and commissioned photography © Ryland Peters & Small, 2016. For full picture credits, see page 127.

All attempts to clear the rights of images used in this book and a diligent search has been undertaken by the publisher. If you know of, or are, the rights holder of any of the works in this book, please contact us via email – info@rps.co.uk.

Notes

When using slices of citrus fruits, try to find organic, unwaxed fruits and wash well before using. if you can only find treated fruit, scrub well in warm soapy water and rinse well before using

Both British (Metric) and American (imperial) are included in these recipes for your convenience, however it is important to work with one set of measurements and not alternate within a recipe.

Measurements are occasionally given in barspoons, which are equivalent to 5 ml/1 teaspoon.

Please drink responsibly.

The authors' moral rights have been asserted. All rights reserved. No part of this publication may be reproduced, stored in a retrieval system or transmitted in any form or by any means, electronic, mechanical, photocopying or otherwise, without the prior permission of the publisher.

A CIP record for this book is available from the British Library. US Library of Congress CIP data has been applied for.

ISBN: 978-1-84975-716-4

Printed in China

Contents

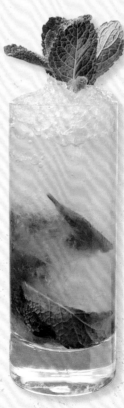

Introduction

Cuba: home of cigars, soulful music, classic American cars, stunning beaches and... RUM!

Nowhere in the world makes cocktails quite like Cuba – known as the 'Isle of Rum' – and nowhere in Cuba serves cocktails quite like its capital city, Havana. A cocktail Mecca, this vibrant city is the birthplace of many world-class creations, like the Cuba Libre, Daiquiri, El Presidente and Mojito. The supreme quality of the rum and the passionate creativity of the local bartenders are to thank for the party in the mouth that kicks off with every delightfully delicious sip. The Cuban bar scene has been on a roll since 1924, when 'El Club de Cantineros' (The Cuban Bartenders' Club) was set up. This elite society opened a cocktail school, which taught aspiring bartenders how to mix drinks expertly and become the perfect hosts. They were likened to symphony conductors: multilingual, well-read, and with a repertoire of over 200 cocktails to boot. In 1935, the club's first cocktail competition was hosted and, since then, Havana has seen mixologists flock from all over the world to battle it out for the ultimate accolade as the ruler of rum. The animated energy of Havana is infectious – it'll scoop you up and carry you along on a sea of rum and fun to a place where you'll dance 'til dawn, laugh 'til you cry and your mojo will raise the roof. Be transported to this happy place by shaking, sloshing and shimmying these rum-based cocktails that exude Cuba's spicy culture with gutsy gusto.

Time flies when you're having rum...

1493: Christopher Columbus introduces sugarcane into the New World.

1620: The first distillation of rum takes place on the sugarcane plantations of the Caribbean when slaves discover that molasses, a by-product of sugar refining, can be fermented into alcohol.

1655: The British Royal Navy changes the daily ration of liquor given to sailors from French brandy to rum, following the capture of Jamaica, where rum is domestically produced.

1664: The first rum distillery in North America is set up on what is now Staten Island in New York.

1667: The manufacture of rum becomes early Colonial New England's greatest and most prosperous industry.

1700s: Cuba is the world's main supplier of rum.

1703: Mount Gay, now the oldest existing rum company in the world, is set up in Barbados.

1739: Rum is used in the slave trade as currency. The slave Venture Smith is purchased in Africa for four gallons of rum and a piece of calico (cotton cloth).

1763: There are now 159 rum distilleries in New England alone.

1774: Before the American Revolutionary War, it's estimated that people are drinking an average of 14 litres/quarts of rum every year.

1789: First president of the United States, George Washington, insists on a barrel of Barbados rum at his inauguration.

1800s: Thanks to Pedro Diago – the 'Father of Cuban Rum' – the quality of rum improves dramatically due to the introduction of copper stills and the first attempts at ageing the drink.

1850: 'Ron Superior Rum' is developed following the Spanish monarchy's request for a delicate, more refined rum that can 'satisfy the court and the elite of the Empire'.

1860: There are more than 1,000 distilleries in Cuba due to the popularity of Ron Superior's smooth, crisp flavour.

1862: Bacardi, now the largest privately held, family-owned spirits company in the world, is founded.

1920 to 1933: 'Dry laws' in America prohibit alcohol from being sold or consumed, encouraging parched tourists to head to Havana. Liquor is also brought over illegally by rum-runners to 'Rum Rows' located near major US ports.

1924: 'El Club de Cantineros' (The Cuban Bartenders' Club) is set up.

1929: The Festival of the Cantinero is started, where bartenders from around the world gather in Havana.

1934: Rum brand Havana Club is created in Cuba.

1935: The Club de Cantineros's first cocktail competition is hosted.

1960: While drinking daiquiris over dinner on election night, John F. Kennedy learns that he will be the next president of the United States.

1970: The practice of giving its sailors a daily rum ration, or 'tot', is abolished by the British Royal Navy.

1996: The first Havana Club International Cocktail Grand Prix takes place in Havana, attracting top mixologists from around the globe.

2003 to 2005: Rum sales in America grow 23 per cent to $1.8 billion.

2003: 'Why is the rum gone?' becomes a famous quote said by Captain Jack Sparrow, played by Johnny Depp, in *Pirates of the Caribbean: The Curse of the Black Pearl*.

2011: Rum brand Captain Morgan changes its slogan to 'To Life, Love and Loot'.

2012: The global consumption of rum is 1.47 billion litres/quarts – almost more than the amount of Scotch whisky, gin and tequila combined.

2013: Due to a craze for mojitos, rum cocktails are more popular than vodka cocktails for the first time since the '60s.

2014: Sixteen bottles of 234-year-old rum are discovered in stately home Harewood House in Leeds, UK, and sold for £135,000 ($200,000). That's more than £8,000 ($11,000) a bottle.

Become a Cuban Bartender

Cuba's 'Maestro Roneros' (master rum-makers) are in training for around 15 years before they are considered 'true' Maestro Roneros. Who has that kind of time? This 15-minute crash course will equip you with all you need to craft Cuban concoctions with creative clout.

Getting into the Spirit

Almost all types of rum are aged in oak barrels that previously held whiskey or bourbon, but some are held in other wooden drums or stainless steel tanks. The amount of time the rum spends in the barrel will define the drink's flavour and hue. When aged in wood, it becomes dark; when aged in stainless steel, the rum remains almost colourless. When they're ready, the rums are blended (often with rums from different stills, ages, barrel types and countries) to a brand's own unique recipe.

Dark Rum Aged in charred oak barrels for a minimum of three years, the liquid reacts with the wood and draws in the flavour, turning from clear to golden and ultimately dark brown. Dark rums taste intense, rich and spicy, and often contain a strong molasses or caramel overtone.

Light/White/Silver Rum Light rums have a shorter ageing process, spending one to two years in a white oak barrel (then filtered to make it clear) or a stainless steel tank. Most light rums have a slightly sweet, yet dry, flavour. Their milder taste makes them perfect in cocktails.

Golden Rum Somewhere between light and dark, golden rums are great in cocktails but smooth enough to be supped neat. Also known as 'amber rum', this medium-bodied liquid is generally fruity with a sweet edge – think a touch of honey, caramel or toffee.

Spiced Rum Laced with zing, spiced rum is infused with herbs and spices – such as cinnamon, pepper, aniseed and rosemary – to create a flavourful drink that leaves a tingle on the tongue.

Flavoured Rum Often infused with fruity flavours such as coconut, mango, apple, orange, banana or lime, flavoured rums are usually less than 40 per cent alcohol (80 proof).

Cuban Essentials

Measure Measures come in many sizes. The dual measure – where one end holds a single shot and the other holds a double – is a good buy.

Shaker Shake your money-maker with either the three-piece (deco) shaker or the Boston shaker. The three-piece is more suitable for home creations, whereas bartenders prefer the Boston because it allows more volume.

Strainer There are two types of strainer: the Hawthorn strainer that sits over the metal part of the shaker, and the Julep that fits in the mixing glass.

Barspoon With its long handle, this is used for the gentle pouring needed to layer cocktails. The flat end can be used to crush, or muddle.

Muddler If more intensive muddling is required – say, you need to extract the juice from fruit – a muddler (pestle) will do the trick.

Pourer A pourer allows liquid to be tipped at a regulated rate. In place of a measure, bartenders count to a fixed number when pouring, bearing in mind that liquors pour at different speeds depending on their sugar content.

Straws To test the balance of your drink, dip a straw into it and place your finger over the top to create a vacuum. Take the straw out and taste the liquid to determine if you need to add anything.

Swizzle Stick A two-pronged stick for stirring drinks that have been 'built' in the glass.

Ice Cubed ice will melt (diluting the drink) at a slower rate but will also chill a cocktail less effectively. Drinks using crushed ice are more plentiful these days owing to the popularity of cocktails like the Mojito. Shaved ice is mostly used in drinks that require dilution to make them more palatable, and where they need to be as cold as possible.

Glassware

Shot Glass This glass holds either a single or a double shot and is used to serve shooters.

Old Fashioned Glass Also known as a Rocks Glass or Tumbler, this is used for short drinks on the rocks.

Highball Glass A tall, thin glass used to serve long cocktails that often need topping up.

Heatproof Glass These come in all shapes and sizes – from a wine-glass-shaped Irish-coffee glass to a tall latte glass.

Champagne Flute With its long stem and narrow rim, the champagne flute will keep your bubbly sparkling for as long as it it in the glass.

Martini Glass This glass has a cone-shaped bowl and a long stem.

Coupette Glass Similar to a martini glass but larger and curved.

Hurricane Glass Inspired by the rum-based Hurricane cocktail, this glass will blow you away! Also known as a Tulip Glass, it holds punches and frozen drinks.

Techniques

Let's talk about six, baby! That is, the six basic techniques behind the creation of a cocktail...

1. Building This is the process of pouring a drink into a glass, one ingredient after another. It's the technique you'd use to make a tall drink such as a Cuba Libre (see page 76). When building a drink, add as much ice to the glass as possible and, once 'built', stir with a barspoon.

2. Stirring When all the ingredients in a drink are alcoholic, the best method of mixing and chilling them is stirring. If you have time, chill the glass first by adding ice and stirring with a barspoon (make sure any dilution is discarded before the alcohol is added), or place the glass in the freezer for an hour prior to making the drink. When stirring a drink, place your spoon in the glass and gently stir the ice continuously. Add all the ingredients and stir until the liquid is as cold as it can be.

3. Muddling Muddling ingredients may require a barspoon or a muddler, depending on the intensity of muddling needed.

So whether releasing the flavour of a herb (such as mint in a Mojito, see page 65), extracting the juices of a fruit (such as the lemon and lime in The Knickerbocker, see pages 32–33) or dissolving something into a liquid (such as sugar into a Piña Colada, see page 86–87), the tool may change but the method is the same.

4. Blending Blending a drink is usually required when its ingredients involve heavy dairy products (as in the Piña Colada) or fresh fruit and frozen variations on classic drinks (like the Strawberry Daiquiri). When adding the ice, less is more – add too much and the drink becomes too solid. But be warned, as the ice is crushed, the drink will dilute or separate quickly.

5. Shaking There's a whole lotta shakin' goin' on… particularly with drinks that contain 'heavy' ingredients. When shaking a cocktail, keep one hand at each end of the shaker and shake vertically, allowing the ice and liquid to travel the full distance of the vessel.

6. Layering When layering a cocktail, choose liquors that will look dramatic – there isn't much point in layering liquids of the same colour. Layer each liquid in order of density – add the heaviest spirits first. The lower the alcohol content (ABV) and the greater the sugar level, the denser the liquid. Therefore, the sweetest and lowest ABV liquid should be poured into the glass first. Then pour the second liquid down the spiral stem of a barspoon with the flat bottom resting on the surface of the liquid below.

Tips and Tricks

Chilling Glasses Fill a glass with ice and leave until it feels very cold. Discard the ice before pouring the cocktail into the glass.

Squeezing Citrus Fruit If the fruit feels hard, 'massage' it in your hands before squeezing it as this helps to extract the juice.

Salt and Sugar Rims Rub the rim of a glass with a wedge of citrus fruit to create a sticky surface. Hold the glass upside-down so the juice doesn't run down the sides of the glass. Dip the rim in salt or sugar.

Twist This usually refers to a strip of citrus peel about 5 cm/2 inches long. Use a vegetable peeler or paring knife to remove the peel, being careful not to include any pith. It's easier if you use fruits with thick skins.

Flaming A piece of citrus peel is held at one end and a lighter brought up to it. The peel is then held over the glass and twisted to create a fine, aromatic mist that falls onto the top of the cocktail.

Sugar Syrup Put 1½ parts superfine/caster sugar and 1 part water in a saucepan and heat gently, stirring, until the sugar is dissolved. Don't allow it to boil or it will become too thick. Allow to cool completely and store in a bottle in the fridge for up to three months. For a Dark Sugar Syrup, substitute the superfine/caster sugar in the method for Sugar Syrup (above) for half demerara/turbinado sugar and half dark muscovado sugar. For a Honey Syrup, substitute the superfine/caster sugar for runny honey.

Hard Ice 'Hard' ice takes longer to melt than ordinary ice, so dilutes the cocktail at a slower rate. Machine-made 'hard' ice is double- or triple-frozen. To make it at home, freeze a sheet of ice cubes. Once frozen, remove from the freezer and allow to thaw, then refreeze. Repeat. For crushed ice, wrap ice cubes in a kitchen cloth and bash with a rolling pin.

RUM-DINGERS

★

Shorts and Shooters

Original Daiquiri

★

The daiquiri was made famous by Ernest Hemingway's favourite bartender at El Floridita bar, Constantino Ribalaigua. Sometime around 1920, after experimenting with various ingredients and techniques, 'El Grande Constante' – as Hemingway called him – finally got the texture of the ice just right. El Floridita has been calling itself 'La Cuna del Daiquiri' (The Cradle of the Daiquiri) ever since.

50 ML/1³/₄ OZ. GOLDEN RUM

20 ML/³/₄ OZ. FRESH LIME JUICE

10 ML/2 BARSPOONS SUGAR SYRUP (SEE PAGE 17)

Pour all the ingredients into an ice-filled shaker.
Shake and strain into a chilled martini glass.

Orange Daiquiri

Sixty per cent of Cuba's citrus produce is oranges. Squeeze every ounce of pleasure out of this cocktail as you imagine the bright, juicy fruits piled high in local Cuban markets, strung up by the roadside or looped over long sticks carried by vendors.

50 ML/1³/₄ OZ. CREOLE SHRUBB RUM

12.5 ML/2¹/₂ BARSPOONS FRESH LEMON JUICE

5 ML/1 BARSPOON SUGAR SYRUP (SEE PAGE 17)

Pour all the ingredients into an ice-filled shaker.
Shake and strain into a chilled martini glass.

Strawberry Daiquiri

Settle in for the evening with a Strawberry Daiquiri and a screening of *Strawberry & Chocolate*, an Oscar-nominated Cuban film that makes a strong political point. The title signifies ice-cream flavours: the pink strawberry being a metaphor for homosexuality and originality, the brown chocolate being the slog of life controlled by the state. Although it may not sound like it, it's actually a witty comedy and received rave reviews.

2 STRAWBERRiES, PLUS 1 SLiCED
STRAWBERRY, TO GARNiSH

125 ML/4 OZ. RUM

50 ML/1¾ OZ. FRESH LiME JUiCE

50 ML/1¾ OZ. SUGAR SYRUP
(SEE PAGE 17)

Muddle the strawberries in a Boston shaker, add the other ingredients and shake with ice. Fine-strain into a chilled cocktail glass and garnish with a sliced strawberry fan.

Dry Daiquiri

During Prohibition – when the U.S. imposed 'dry laws' – Facundito Bacardi, the founder of the brand, invited Americans to 'Come to Cuba and bathe in Bacardi rum'. Prohibition may be over but you can still bathe in this delicious Dry Daiquiri.

110 ML/3½ OZ. RUM

35 ML/1¼ OZ. SUGAR SYRUP (SEE PAGE 17)

50 ML/1¾ OZ. FRESH LIME JUICE

15 ML/½ OZ. CAMPARI

A DASH OF PASSIONFRUIT SYRUP

ORANGE TWIST, TO GARNISH

Shake all the ingredients with ice and fine-strain into a chilled cocktail glass. Squeeze the zest from the orange twist over the surface of the drink and add to the glass to garnish.

Hemingway Daiquiri

Legend has it that Ernest Hemingway once consumed 16 of these daiquiris in one sitting – modified from the original recipe by the man himself – in his favourite Havana bar, El Floridita. He's still there, in fact, propping up the bar, immortalized in bronze.

50 ML/1³/₄ OZ. LIGHT PUERTO RICAN-STYLE RUM

20 ML/³/₄ OZ. FRESH GRAPEFRUIT JUICE

10 ML/2 BARSPOONS FRESH LIME JUICE

10 ML/2 BARSPOONS MARASCHINO LIQUEUR

LEMON PEEL, TO GARNISH

Add all the ingredients to a cocktail shaker filled with ice and shake sharply to mix. Strain into a chilled coupette glass and serve garnished with lemon peel.

Commodore Cocktail

Partly set at the Guantanamo Bay Naval Base in Cuba, courtroom drama *A Few Good Men* is the perfect film to watch as you sip a Commodore. Just try not to choke on the rich, frothy liquid as Jack Nicholson declares, 'You can't handle the truth!'

50 ML/1¾ OZ. LIGHT PUERTO RICAN-STYLE RUM

25 ML/1 OZ. FRESH LEMON JUICE

10 ML/2 BARSPOONS GRENADINE

10 ML/2 BARSPOONS RASPBERRY SYRUP (SEE PAGE 32)

5 G/1 BARSPOON CASTER/SUPERFINE SUGAR

1 EGG WHITE

Add all ingredients to a cocktail shaker filled with ice and shake sharply to blend and whip up the egg white. Strain into a frosted coupette glass and serve immediately while the froth is still at its best.

Bacardi Cocktail

Have you ever wondered why Bacardi bottles feature a bat? As bats are a symbol of good fortune, when Doña Amalia Bacardí spotted fruit bats in the rafters of her family's distillery, she insisted the winged creature become part of the logo.

50 ML/1³/₄ OZ. BACARDI WHITE RUM

A DASH OF GRENADINE

FRESH JUICE OF 1 SMALL LIME

1 BARSPOON ICING/CONFECTIONERS' SUGAR OR A DASH OF SUGAR SYRUP (SEE PAGE 17)

Shake all the ingredients sharply over ice, then strain into a frosted martini glass and serve.

Bacardi rum was originally produced in Cuba but, after the Cuban Revolution, the brand was forced to move to Puerto Rico and start up again from scratch.

Cubanada

There's 'nada' more delectable than the sweet taste of maple syrup with golden rum! Those with pronounced oak flavours and full-bodied English Island rums, like ones from Jamaica, will work particularly well in this cocktail. If you use a lighter-bodied rum, perhaps cut the maple syrup down to 1 part and add the equivalent amount of sugar syrup.

125 ML/4 OZ. RUM

50 ML/1³/₄ OZ. MAPLE SYRUP

50 ML/1³/₄ OZ. FRESH LIME JUICE

2 DASHES OF ANGOSTURA BITTERS

LIME SLICE, TO GARNISH

Shake all the ingredients with ice and fine-strain into a chilled cocktail glass. Garnish with a thin lime wheel on the rim of the glass.

Ambrosia

Ambrosia was the nectar of the gods and, with Cuba's 160,000 beehives producing lovely, sticky honey, this flavourful drink will leave you buzzing.

125 ML/4 OZ. CUBAN RUM

50 ML/1¾ OZ. HONEY SYRUP (SEE PAGE 17)

50 ML/1¾ OZ. FRESH LIME JUICE

2 DASHES OF ANGOSTURA BITTERS

ORANGE TWIST, TO GARNISH

Shake all the ingredients with ice and fine-strain into a chilled cocktail glass. Squeeze the zest from the orange twist over the surface of the drink and add to the glass as a garnish.

The Knickerbocker

The term 'knickerbocker' refers to a New Yorker. While Rat-Packer Sammy Davis Jr. was born in Harlem, his roots came from his African-American and Afro-Cuban parents. Listen to his toe-tapping *New York's My Home* as you enjoy this lip-smacking punch.

50 ML/1¾ OZ. SANTA CRUZ RUM

25 ML/1 OZ. ORANGE CURAÇAO

20 ML/¾ OZ. FRESH LEMON JUICE

15 ML/½ OZ. FRESH LIME JUICE

FRESH RASPBERRIES, TO GARNISH

RASPBERRY SYRUP

8 FRESH RASPBERRIES

150 ML/⅔ CUP SUGAR SYRUP (SEE PAGE 17)

To make the raspberry syrup, put the raspberries in a mixing glass or bowl and press them gently with the back of a spoon to release the juice. Cover with sugar syrup and leave overnight to infuse.

Pass the syrup through a fine mesh sieve/strainer and discard the raspberry pulp and seeds.

Add 10 ml/2 barspoons of the raspberry syrup to a cocktail shaker with the rum and curaçao and fill with ice. Squeeze in the juice from the lemon and lime, and drop the spent husks in too. Shake the mixture together.

Strain the drink into a stemmed cocktail glass and serve garnished with fresh raspberries.

Rum Sombrero

Tia Maria is a rum-based coffee liqueur with an intriguing history dating back to the 17th century. Legend has it that a beautiful Spanish aristocrat fled the Caribbean island of Jamaica due to the colonial wars, leaving behind all her possessions. Her brave maid, however, saved one family treasure: a jewellery box containing a pair of black pearl earrings and an ancient manuscript holding the recipe for a liqueur. This liqueur was named after the courageous maid: Tia Maria.

100 ML/3½ OZ. RUM

50 ML/1¾ OZ. TiA MARiA

25 ML/1 OZ. ESPRESSO

A DASH OF DARK SUGAR SYRUP (SEE PAGE 17)

50 ML/1¾ OZ. DOUBLE/HEAVY CREAM, LiGHTLY WHiPPED

COFFEE BEANS OR PiNCH OF GROUND CiNNAMON, TO GARNiSH

Shake the first four ingredients with ice and strain into a chilled cocktail glass. Float the lightly whipped cream on top and garnish with three coffee beans or a pinch of ground cinnamon.

The most expensive rum in the world is owned by Jamaican brand Wray & Nephew. Containing blends that are believed to date as far back as 1915, there are four bottles remaining and can be bought for £26,000/$40,000 a pop.

Mulata Daisy

★

This inventive creation won the UK's 2009 Bacardi Legacy Cocktail Competition. It's described as a 'modern interpretation of one of the most classic of the Bacardi cocktails, the Daiquiri.' It has been said to conjure the image of a Cuban flower girl swaying her hips as she walks down the street.

20 ML/¾ OZ. FRESH LIME JUICE

1–2 TABLESPOONS COCOA POWDER

10 ML/2 BARSPOONS GALLIANO LIQUEUR

5 ML/1 BARSPOON CASTER/SUPERFINE SUGAR

1 TEASPOON FENNEL SEEDS

40 ML/1¼ OZ. BARCARDI RUM

20 ML/¾ OZ. CHOCOLATE LIQUEUR

Before juicing the lime, halve it and run a cut surface round the rim of the glass, then carefully dip the rim into cocoa powder to create a soft, chocolatey 'collar'.

Swirl the inside of the glass with the Galliano liqueur, which will give a final bouquet of aniseed and other fresh aromas. Stir the sugar and lime juice together in a shaker; add the fennel seeds and muddle them gently with a stirrer. Add ice, the rum and chocolate liqueur. Shake vigorously. Double-strain into a coupe glass.

Malecón

Named after an esplanade in Havana, this cocktail was designed by mixologist Erik Lorincz in 2007. 'I wanted to create a drink that could be enjoyed at any time of day or night, and that would be at home in the most elegant London cocktail bar and equally at the Malecón in Havana with music, laughter and tobacco smoke in the air,' he says.

30 ML/1 OZ. FRESH LiME JUiCE

2 TEASPOONS CASTER/SUPERFiNE SUGAR

3 DROPS OF PEYCHAUD'S BiTTERS

50 ML/2 OZ. BACARDi WHiTE RUM

10 ML/2 BARSPOONS OLOROSO SHERRY

15 ML/½ OZ. RUBY PORT

Pre-chill a glass with ice. Pour the lime juice over ice in a shaker. Add the rest of the ingredients. Shake. Strain into the glass (having discarded the ice used for chilling). To serve, add a single lump of ice.

Air Mail

In 1930, the Cuban government started its regular airmail service on the island, which was a big deal, especially as they'd been working on it for around 15 years. It wasn't long before the Air Mail cocktail appeared in a Bacardi promotional leaflet and, charmingly, bartenders used to attach airmail stamps to the glass as a garnish.

25 ML/1 OZ. GOLD PUERTO RICAN-STYLE RUM

12.5 ML/2½ BARSPOONS FRESH LIME JUICE

5 ML/1 BARSPOON RUNNY HONEY

CHAMPAGNE, TO TOP UP

Add the rum, lime juice and honey to a cocktail shaker and stir until the honey is dissolved. Add ice and shake to mix. Strain into a Champagne flute, top up with Champagne and serve.

Bazooka Joe

Named after the American comic-strip character featured inside the wrappers of bubblegum Bazooka, this colourful, layered shot tells a sweet story.

1 PART BANANA LiQUEUR

1 PART BLUE CURAÇAO

1 PART BAiLEYS

Layer the ingredients in the order listed but be a little careful with the first layer, as different brands of curaçao and banana liqueur have different densities. You may need to switch their order around, so make a small test drink to start with.

June Bug

Cuba's streets are packed with vintage cars from the 1950s, with the Volkswagen Beetle – or Bug – nipping between Chevrolets, Dodges, Studebakers and Chryslers. Get your engine revving with this bright shooter, which also makes a great long drink if one shot isn't enough. Simply multiply the ingredients by four and serve over ice in a highball glass.

1 PART COCONUT RUM

1 PART MiDORi MELON LiQUEUR

1 PART PiNEAPPLE JUiCE

A SQUEEZE OF FRESH LiME

Shake all the ingredients together with ice and strain into a large shot glass. If made properly, the drink will have a nice frothy head.

Paradise Punch

The Caribbean island of Cuba – punctuated by its scattering of archipelagos – is nothing short of paradise. This tropical blend of exotic juices will carry you to utopia, awash with white-sand beaches, swaying palm trees and dive-right-in waters.

1 PART TROPICAL JUICE MIX

¼ PART DARK RUM

¼ PART WHITE RUM

¼ PART AGED RUM

¼ PART MARASCHINO LIQUEUR

¼ PART LIME JUICE

A DASH OF GRENADINE

Make a mix of your favourite tropical juices; guava, pineapple, mango and passionfruit are a good start. Shake all the ingredients, apart from the grenadine, and pour into a shot glass. Drop a little grenadine into the glass and swirl until you get a perfect sunset effect.

Surfer on Acid

For political reasons, surfing in Cuba was banned for many years as the government was concerned that people would try to paddle to Florida. Thankfully, this law has been lifted and, despite a lack of access to surfing equipment (some gnarly die-hards still ride the waves on makeshift boards made from refrigerator doors!), the Cuban surf scene is gaining momentum. Knock back this shot as you declare, 'Surf's up, dude!'

1 PART COCONUT RUM
½ PART PINEAPPLE JUICE
½ PART JÄGERMEISTER

Stir the first two ingredients together with ice until chilled (if you shake it, you will get too much froth). Float the Jägermeister on the top. Traditionally, this shot is consumed from the bottom with a straw, so you finish with a hit of Jäger.

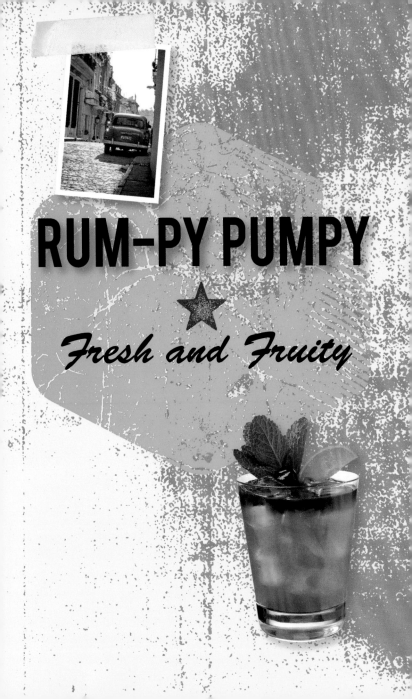

RUM-PY PUMPY

★

Fresh and Fruity

Colonel Beach's Plantation Punch

⭐

Created in the 1950s by 'Don the Beachcomber' to be served in his restaurant The Colonel Plantation Beef Steak and Coffee House, this experimental blend of unusual ingredients is pretty punchy.

25 ML/1 OZ. GOLD CUBAN RUM

50 ML/1¾ OZ. GOLD JAMAICAN RUM

25 ML/1 OZ. GOLD BARBADIAN RUM

25 ML/1 OZ. FRESH LIME JUICE

50 ML/1¾ OZ. GINGER BEER

50 ML/1¾ OZ. PINEAPPLE JUICE

2 DASHES OF ANGOSTURA BITTERS

2 DASHES OF FALERNUM

2 DASHES OF PERNOD

ORANGE SLICES, COCKTAIL CHERRIES AND
FRESH MINT SPRIGS, TO GARNISH

Add all the ingredients to a cocktail shaker filled with ice and shake together to mix. Pour into an ice-filled Tiki mug (if you have one) or glass, and serve garnished with an orange slice, cocktail cherry and a mint sprig, held together with a toothpick.

Planter's Punch

While the origins of this drink are disputed, one claim is that it was the creation of a planter's wife, who mixed it to cool down the workers on a Caribbean plantation after a day's toil. If it wasn't for such workers, rum may never have existed as it was they who discovered that molasses, a by-product of sugar-refining, could be fermented into alcohol.

50 ML/1³⁄₄ OZ. LIGHT PUERTO RICAN-STYLE RUM

50 ML/1³⁄₄ OZ. FRESH ORANGE JUICE

30 ML/1 OZ. FRESH LEMON JUICE

15 ML/¹⁄₂ OZ. GRENADINE

25 ML/1 OZ. SODA WATER

10 ML/2 BARSPOONS DARK JAMAICAN RUM

ORANGE SLICES AND COCKTAIL CHERRIES, TO GARNISH

Add the light rum, orange and lemon juices and grenadine to a cocktail shaker and shake together. Pour into a highball glass filled with crushed ice and top up with soda. Gently pour the dark rum over the surface – it should float naturally on top, while the grenadine should sink to the bottom. Serve garnished with an orange slice and a cocktail cherry, held together with a toothpick.

Bay Breeze

★

This uncomplicated and refreshing drink is an International Bartenders Association (IBA) official cocktail. This means that it can be used in the annual bartending World Cocktail Competition, making it one of the most frequently made cocktails by expert mixologists across the globe.

50 ML/1³/₄ OZ. GOLDEN RUM

100 ML/3¹/₂ OZ. CRANBERRY JUICE

50 ML/1³/₄ OZ. PINEAPPLE JUICE

LIME WEDGE, TO GARNISH

Add all the ingredients to a shaker filled with ice, shake and strain into a highball glass filled with ice. Garnish with a lime wedge and serve.

Admiral Nelson, who died in the Battle of Trafalgar, loved rum so much that his body was preserved in a barrel of the beverage before he was laid to rest. It was later discovered that a hole had been drilled into the bottom of the barrel so that the sailors could drink the rum during its transit back to England. Hence why rum was referred to as 'Nelson's Blood'.

Mai Tai

There's great debate as to who first concocted the Mai Tai – either 'Don the Beachcomber' (see page 49) or 'Trader Vic'. Trader Vic spent much time in Cuba refining his bartending skills and knowledge of rum, while Don the Beachcomber travelled around many Caribbean islands before opening his first bar in Hollywood. Regardless of who dreamt up the Mai Tai, they probably both agreed that it tastes 'very good', which is its Tahitian translation.

100 ML/3½ OZ. GOLD RUM

50 ML/1¾ OZ. ORANGE CURAÇAO

25 ML/1 OZ. ORGEAT (ALMOND) SYRUP

50 ML/1¾ OZ. FRESH LIME JUICE

A DASH OF ANGOSTURA BITTERS

25 ML/1 OZ. DARK RUM

MINT SPRIG, TO GARNISH

Shake the first five ingredients with ice and strain into a large rocks glass over cubed ice. Gently float the dark rum over the surface and then garnish with the mint sprig.

Frozen Kiwi Daiquiri

Kiwi photographer Maureen Tan left her New Zealand home and spent two months living in Cuba. She immersed herself in Havana's culture in order to capture life behind the city's jazz, rum and vintage cars. 'We were invited into people's homes and learned about their lives,' she says. The result: insightful, thought-provoking images that were displayed at Auckland's Festival of Photography. In homage to her efforts, try this frozen version of a classic Daiquiri, spiked with kiwi purée and a fresh kiwi garnish.

340 G/12 OZ. FROZEN LEMONADE CONCENTRATE, THAWED

170 G/6 OZ. FROZEN LIMEADE CONCENTRATE, THAWED

750 ML/¾ QUART LIGHT RUM

500–750 ML/2–3 CUPS KIWI PURÉE

LIME WEDGES OR KIWI SLICES, TO GARNISH

SERVES 20

Combine all the ingredients, except the kiwi purée, with 1 litre/quart water in a large container and freeze for 24 hours. When ready to serve, remove from the freezer and break up with a spoon. Add kiwi purée to taste and stir. Serve in your choice of well-chilled glass, garnished as desired.

Rum Runner

⭐

This cocktail is criminally delicious. During Prohibition, from 1920 to 1933, rum-running – the act of smuggling forbidden alcohol across a border – was rife. It began with cheap Caribbean rum being transported to Florida speakeasies and progressed to Canadian whisky, French Champagne and English gin being delivered to major cities like New York and Boston. Some ships were said to have carried $200,000 (£130,000) in contraband in a single run.

25 ML/1 OZ. WHITE RUM

25 ML/1 OZ. DARK RUM

FRESH JUICE OF 1 LIME

A DASH OF SUGAR SYRUP (SEE PAGE 17)

150 ML/²/₃ CUP PINEAPPLE JUICE

Shake all the ingredients sharply over ice in a shaker and strain into a highball glass filled with crushed ice.

Officer's Nightcap

Fancy a nightcap? Perhaps you'd like a cigar to accompany your snifter? Cuban cigars have a reputation as the finest in the world due to their superior tobacco and precise care and attention that goes into each one. It takes over 100 steps to properly produce a single Cuban cigar but, as ridiculous folklore would have you believe, being rolled on the thighs of a virgin is not one of them.

25 ML/1 OZ. FRESH LIME JUICE

10 ML/2 BARSPOONS VELVET FALERNUM

15 ML/½ OZ. AGAVE SYRUP

15 ML/½ OZ. RON ZACAPA DARK RUM

60 ML/2 OZ. APPLE JUICE

10 ML/2 BARSPOONS PIMENTO DRAM LIQUEUR

LIME TWIST AND CINNAMON STICKS, TO GARNISH

First, fill a highball glass with ice and set aside. Add all the ingredients to a shaker. Give a quick stir and top up with ice. Shake. Strain any melted water from the glass but leave the ice in it. Strain the cocktail into the glass and garnish with the lime twist and cinnamon.

RUM AND RUMMER

★

Long and Strong

Mojito

One of the world's most popular cocktails, the fresh, minty Mojito was famously enjoyed by novelist Ernest Hemingway at La Bodeguita del Medio bar in Havana, a bar still frequented by many cocktail drinkers today.

8 MINT LEAVES

125 ML/4 OZ. CUBAN RUM

50 ML/1³/₄ OZ. FRESH LIME JUICE

50 ML/1³/₄ OZ. SUGAR SYRUP (SEE PAGE 17)

MINT SPRIGS, TO GARNISH

Gently muddle the mint leaves in a large highball glass. Add the other ingredients and swizzle with crushed ice. Garnish with a mint sprig to serve.

Minty fresh:

The mint garnish is so important with this drink. Use a healthy bushel of mint to make the drink look great and to encourage a fragrant aroma.

American novelist Ernest Hemingway wrote 'For Whom the Bell Tolls' and 'The Old Man and the Sea' while he lived in Cuba.

Raspberry and Rose Mojito

While the rosy hue of this cocktail can't help but lift your spirits, pink also makes a point. As reported by *Pink News*, in May 2015, a mass wedding was arranged in Cuba to push for legal recognition of same-sex marriages, as part of the country's annual gay pride parade.

15 ML/½ OZ. ROSE SYRUP

8 MiNT LEAVES

50 ML/2 OZ. LiGHT RUM

FRESH JUiCE OF 1 LiME

15 ML/½ OZ. CRÈME DE FRAMBOiSE (RASPBERRY LiQUEUR)

2 ROSE PETALS AND A MiNT SPRiG, TO GARNiSH

Pour the rose syrup into a highball glass. Add the mint leaves and rum. Delicately press the mint with the back of a barspoon – you want to extract the flavour without breaking up the leaves. Add the lime juice and enough ice to come two-thirds of the way up the glass. Gently churn with the spoon. Pile up with more crushed ice and drizzle over the crème de framboise. Garnish with the rose petals and mint before serving.

Havana Club Añejo 7 Años was
the first Cuban rum intended
to be drunk neat. it takes more
than 14 years to create and no
individual rum used in the blend
is less than seven years old.

Anejo Highball

This drink was created in 2000 by master mixologist Dale DeGroff as a tribute to Cuban bartenders of the early 1900s. 'Rum, lime, and Curaçao are the holy trinity of Caribbean cocktails,' he says. Garnished with a lime wheel and orange slice to give a nod to the ingredients within the glass, this is the perfect refresher to cool down with on a hot summer day.

100 ML/3½ OZ. CUBAN RUM

50 ML/1¾ OZ. ORANGE CURAÇAO

50 ML/1¾ OZ. FRESH LIME JUICE

2 DASHES OF ANGOSTURA BITTERS

200 ML/7 OZ. GINGER BEER

LIME WHEEL AND ORANGE SLICE, TO GARNISH

Add the first four ingredients to a highball glass filled with ice. Stir well, top up with ginger beer and garnish with a lime wheel and orange slice. Serve immediately.

Queen's Park Swizzle

This drink is a kind of hybrid between the Daiquiri and the Mojito. The key to the intense flavour is to use a heavier dark sugar syrup, made from less-refined demerara/turbinado sugar, which complements the fuller style of rum. In 1946, this enlivening drink was described as 'the most delightful form of amnesia given out today'.

50 ML/1¾ OZ. GUYANESE RUM (TRY EL DORADO 12-YEAR)

20 ML/¾ OZ. FRESH LIME JUICE

15 ML/½ OZ. DARK SUGAR SYRUP (SEE PAGE 17)

2 DASHES OF ANGOSTURA BITTERS

5 FRESH MINT LEAVES, PLUS A MINT SPRIG, TO GARNISH

Add the rum, lime juice, sugar syrup, Angostura bitters and mint leaves to a highball glass filled with crushed ice. Swizzle by placing a barspoon or small whisk into the glass and swizzling between the palms of your hands until frost appears on the outside of the glass. Serve garnished with a mint sprig.

Jalisco Siesta

Despite the sleepy name, this crisp punch screams: 'WAKE UP!'
It's a variation of the Mojito, using tequila instead of rum, which
combines well with the mint. This cocktail has a kick that'll
invigorate your senses, so any chance of a siesta is utterly dashed.

25 ML/1 OZ. FRESH LEMON JUICE

15 ML/½ OZ. AGAVE SYRUP

5 FRESH MINT LEAVES

50 ML/1¾ OZ. REPOSADO TEQUILA

50 ML/1¾ OZ. GINGER BEER

MINT SPRIGS, TO GARNISH

Add the lemon juice, agave syrup and mint leaves to a highball glass
and muddle gently. Fill the glass with crushed ice and add the tequila and
ginger beer. Stir gently to mix and serve garnished with a mint sprig.

Dark and Stormy

⭐

Add fresh strawberries to a Dark and Stormy cocktail to lighten the heavier rum flavour. The succulent strawberries will go a long way to sweeten the drink and – high in antioxidants – will give your body a boost, too.

50 ML/1¾ OZ. DARK RUM

3 LIME WEDGES

2 STRAWBERRIES, SLICED

GINGER BEER, TO TOP UP

Muddle the lime and the strawberries in a highball glass. Add ice and the remaining ingredients and stir gently. Serve immediately.

One legendary Jamaican rum popular in the '60s was so strong that it was nicknamed 'Rude to Your Parents'.

Cuba Libre

Translated as 'Free Cuba', the Cuba Libre is said to have originated in 1900 in Havana when Captain Russell of the U.S. Army ordered a Bacardi rum with a Coca-Cola and a slice of lime to celebrate the U.S. victory over Spain in Cuba. He raised his glass and toasted: 'Por Cuba libre!'

125 ML/4 OZ. CUBAN RUM

35 ML/1¼ OZ. FRESH LIME JUICE

250 ML/1 CUP CARBONATED COLA (SEE OPPOSITE)

LIME WEDGES, TO GARNISH

Build all the ingredients over cubed ice in a highball glass and garnish with two lime wedges to serve.

Rum was thought once to have medicinal properties: the British Navy gave rations of rum, mixed with wine and lime, to its sailors to lessen the risk of scurvy (little did they know that it was actually the lime that was to thank!)

Homemade Cola Cordial

Due to the trade embargo between the U.S. and Cuba enforced by the Fidel Castro government in the 1960s, 99.9 per cent of Cubans have never tried Coca-Cola. Even though you've probably knocked back more Cokes than you can recall, brewing up your very own homemade cola will add a satisfying fizz to your life.

200 G/1 CUP WHITE SUGAR

200 G/1 CUP DARK MUSCOVADO SUGAR

1 VANILLA BEAN/POD, SEEDED

1 CINNAMON STICK

A PINCH OF NUTMEG

PEEL OF 1 ORANGE

PEEL OF 1 LEMON

PEEL OF 1 LIME

CARBONATED WATER, TO SERVE

PEELED CITRUS, TO GARNISH

MAKES ABOUT 200 ML/¾ CUP AND SERVES 8

Put the white and muscovado sugar and 500 ml/2 cups of water in a large saucepan set over medium heat. Simmer gently, stirring frequently, until the sugar has dissolved. Turn down the heat and add the vanilla bean/pod, cinnamon, nutmeg, and zests of the citrus fruit. Allow to simmer for 2 hours over a low heat, stirring occasionally, until reduced to a thin syrup. Leave to cool, pass though a strainer and set aside until needed.

Add the desired amount (relative to sweetness of tooth) to an ice-filled highball glass and top up with 200 ml/¾ cup of carbonated water. Serve garnished with pieces of citrus zest.

If you are not using the cordial immediately, decant into a bottle and store in the refrigerator for up to two days.

Ron Collins

The Ron Collins marches to the beat of its own rum. Based on the Tom Collins but substituting the gin for rum ('ron' in Spanish), it works equally well with light, golden and dark varieties.

125 ML/4 OZ. RUM

75 ML/2½ OZ. SUGAR SYRUP (SEE PAGE 17)

65 ML/2 OZ. FRESH LIME JUICE

150 ML/5 OZ. SODA WATER

3 DASHES OF ANGOSTURA BITTERS

LIME WEDGE, TO GARNISH

Pour the first three ingredients over ice into a highball glass. Top up with soda water, then add the Angostura bitters. Garnish with a lime wedge and serve.

To taste rum 'properly', sip it out of one of the following vessels as they concentrate the aromas: a tulip-shaped sherry copita, a brandy snifter or a white wine glass.

Shelter from the Storm

The original Dark and Stormy cocktail is one of the few trademarked cocktails, and should 'legally' be made with Gosling's Black Seal Rum. This variation adds orange notes from the Curaçao and almond from the orgeat almond-flavoured syrup, and can be made with any aged or dark rum. If you want to 'shelter from the storm', enjoy during the months of June to November – Cuba's hurricane season.

100 ML/3½ OZ. AGED OR DARK RUM

25 ML/1 OZ. ORANGE CURAÇAO OR COINTREAU

25 ML/1 OZ. ORGEAT (ALMOND) SYRUP

50 ML/1¾ OZ. FRESH LIME JUICE

200 ML/7 OZ. GINGER BEER

SLICED GINGER (OPTIONAL) AND LIME WEDGE,
TO GARNISH

Add the first four ingredients to a large highball glass filled with cubed ice and stir. Top up with the ginger beer and garnish with a slice of ginger and a lime wedge to serve.

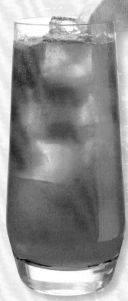

Penzance

Yo-ho-ho and a bottle of rum! Pirates, rum and the sea have been intrinsically linked for centuries. It was only in 1970 that the practice of giving its sailors a daily ration of rum was done away with by the British Royal Navy. Buy yourself a recording of the comic opera *Pirates of Penzance* so you can enjoy this cocktail with the appropriate swashbuckling ambience, me hearty!

40 ML/1½ OZ. BACARDI 8-YEAR-OLD DARK RUM

10 ML/2 BARSPOONS PEACH LIQUEUR

25 ML/1 OZ. FRESH LEMON JUICE

20 ML/¾ OZ. BIRD'S EYE CHILLI/CHILE-INFUSED SUGAR SYRUP

4 FRESH MINT LEAVES

3 DROPS OF ANGOSTURA BITTERS

GINGER BEER, TO TOP UP

FRESH MINT SPRIG, MARINATED CHERRY, AND COMPRESSED PINEAPPLE (VACUUM-PACKED), TO GARNISH

Combine the ingredients in a shaker; fill up with ice. Shake, then double-strain into a glass. Top up with ginger beer. Fill the glass with ice cubes (beware the fizz) and garnish with the mint, cherry and pineapple to serve.

Swizzle

★

When it comes to this drink, it's all in the swizzle, fo' shizzle! The most supreme swizzle can be accomplished with a pronged wooden swizzle stick hailing from the Caribbean island of Martinique. To swizzle effectively, use both hands to spin the stick between your palms as quickly as possible. You'll know you've achieved a proper swizzle if a nice frost is achieved on the outside of the glass.

FRESH JUICE OF ½ LIME

3 DROPS OF THE BITTER TRUTH REPEAL BITTERS

10 ML/2 BARSPOONS PIMENTO DRAM LIQUEUR

50 ML/2 OZ. RON ZACAPA DARK RUM

LIME TWIST AND GRATED TONKA BEAN, TO GARNISH

Combine all the ingredients in a tall glass. Fill three-quarters of the way up with crushed ice. Give a good swizzle. Top up with more crushed ice. To serve, garnish with a lime twist and a few gratings of tonka bean.

80% of the world's rum is made in the Caribbean, with almost every island producing its own unique rum style.

RUM WITH CHUMS

★

Punches and Pitchers

Piña Colada

Country singer Garth Brooks had the right idea when he sang: 'So bring me two piña coladas; One for each hand; Let's set sail with Captain Morgan; And never leave dry land.' Presumably, he was fantasizing about a Piña Colada in his left hand and a Honey Colada in his right. These tropical drinks that taste like sunshine and happiness are sure to give you a 'smile that goes on for miles'.

50 ML/1¾ OZ. GOLDEN RUM

25 ML/1 OZ. COCONUT CREAM

12.5 ML/2½ BARSPOONS DOUBLE/HEAVY CREAM

25 ML/1 OZ. PINEAPPLE JUICE

SLICED PINEAPPLE, TO GARNISH

Put all the ingredients into a blender, add a nice scoop of crushed ice and blend. Pour into a glass and garnish with a thick slice of pineapple to serve.

Honey Colada:
For a sweeter version of this drink, add 10 ml/2 barspoons of honey or sugar syrup (see page 17) to the glass after the drink has been poured.

Iced Piña Colada

Hoist up a hammock and prepare to chill with an Iced Piña Colada. The origin of this sweet, creamy cocktail is contested but many believe it was created in the 1800s by Puerto-Rican pirate, Roberto Cofresi, when he served his crew a blend of rum, coconut and pineapple to boost morale.

300 G/2 CUPS CHOPPED FRESH PINEAPPLE

75 G/6 TABLESPOONS WHITE SUGAR

200 ML/³⁄₄ CUP COCONUT MILK

60 ML/2 OZ. WHITE RUM

SERVES 2

Stir the pineapple with the sugar to mix well. Leave to stand for 10 minutes at room temperature to allow the sugar to dissolve into the chopped pineapple. Put all the ingredients in an ice-cream maker and churn until softly slushy. Pour into chilled glasses and serve immediately.

Tropical Punch

Sing along to Ace of Base's 'Cuba, Cuba Libre' – which goes a little something like this: 'Cuba, Cuba here I come; There's a place in the Caribbean sun; Land of future, land of dreams; Checking for the coast' – as you sip this Tropical Punch and imagine the sun on your face and your toes nestled into the warm sand on one of Cuba's magnificent beaches.

2 LARGE RIPE MANGOS, PEELED, PITTED, AND ROUGHLY CHOPPED

2 SLICES PINEAPPLE, PEELED, CORED, AND ROUGHLY CHOPPED

400 ML/1²⁄₃ CUPS FRESH PINK GRAPEFRUIT JUICE (ABOUT 4 GRAPEFRUITS)

30 ML/1 OZ. FRESH LIME JUICE

A 2.5-CM/1-INCH PIECE OF FRESH GINGER, PEELED

50 ML/SCANT ¼ CUP SUGAR SYRUP (SEE PAGE 17)

MINERAL WATER (STILL OR SPARKLING), TO THIN

PINEAPPLE LEAVES, TO GARNISH

SERVES 2

Add all the ingredients to a blender with a scoop of crushed ice and blitz until smooth. Pour into ice-filled glasses and top up with mineral water to loosen the mixture, if required. Serve garnished with pineapple leaves.

Kingston Cooler

Kingston is the capital of Jamaica, one of Cuba's neighbouring Caribbean islands. Jamaica's most popular rum – Wray & Nephew – is 126 proof. At 63 per cent alcohol content, that makes it the world's most potent rum. A few sips of a Kingston Cooler and you're sure to be feeling 'neighbourly' towards everyone in the room!

500 ML/2 CUPS DARK JAMAICAN RUM

100 ML/⅓ CUP WRAY & NEPHEW OVERPROOF RUM

250 ML/1 CUP FRESH LIME JUICE (ABOUT 8 LIMES)

100 ML/⅓ CUP ORGEAT (ALMOND) SYRUP

500 ML/2 CUPS PASSIONFRUIT JUICE

500 ML/2 CUPS PINEAPPLE JUICE

SEASONAL FRESH FRUIT AND FRESH MINT SPRIGS, TO GARNISH

SERVES 10

Add all the ingredients to a large jug/pitcher or punch bowl filled with ice and stir gently to mix. Serve in ice-filled glasses, garnished with seasonal fruit and mint sprigs.

Cuban Sangria

Add a little olé to your life with this fruity punch – it's especially tasty with Rioja wine. 'Sangria' comes from the Spanish word for blood, 'sangre', a nod to its rich tint. Although traditionally served in Spain and Portugal, Sangria is also common in Peru, Mexico, Puerto Rico, Panama, the Dominican Republic, Chile, Argentina and – yep – Cuba.

750 ML/¾ QUART DRY RED WINE

150 ML/⅔ CUP RUM

250 ML/1 CUP FRESH ORANGE JUICE (ABOUT 4 ORANGES)

50 ML/1¾ OZ. SUGAR SYRUP (SEE PAGE 17)

3 DASHES OF ANGOSTURA BITTERS

SEASONAL FRESH FRUIT, TO GARNISH

SERVES 10

Add all the ingredients to a jug/pitcher filled with ice and stir gently to mix. Serve in ice-filled glasses, garnished with seasonal fruit.

Variation:
For a special occasion, add a bottle of Champagne to the punch bowl to give it extra fizz.

Blanco Sangria

⭐

Celebrate the grapefruit bitters in this drink as you visualize yourself at Cuba's Fiesta de la Toronja — Festival of the Grapefruit — where the residents of Isla de la Juventud (famous for its citrus plantations) celebrate the annual grapefruit harvest.

750 ML/¾ QUART DRY WHITE WINE

100 ML/⅓ CUP ST. GERMAIN ELDERFLOWER LIQUEUR

100 ML/⅓ CUP DRY VERMOUTH

100 ML/⅓ CUP COINTREAU

80 ML/3 OZ. FRESH LEMON JUICE (FROM ABOUT 2 LEMONS)

30 ML/1 OZ. SUGAR SYRUP (SEE PAGE 17), TO TASTE

2 HEAVY DASHES OF GRAPEFRUIT BITTERS

SEASONAL FRESH FRUIT, TO GARNISH

SERVES 10

Add all the ingredients to a jug/pitcher filled with ice and stir gently to mix.

Serve in ice-filled glasses, garnished with seasonal fruit.

Chi Chi

Despite the game's origins in America, baseball is one of the most popular sports in Cuba and is strongly associated with Cuban patriotism. Raise a glass to Chi-Chi Olivo, a Major League baseball pitcher, as you cry, 'Hey, swing, batter batter, swing!' N.B. Don't get 'cream of coconut' confused with 'coconut cream' (which is like coconut milk but with less water), or 'creamed coconut' (which is compressed coconut flesh). The one you're looking for should be sweet – Coco Lopez is a good brand to use.

500 ML/2 CUPS VODKA

1 LITRE/QUART UNSWEETENED PINEAPPLE JUICE

250 ML/1 CUP CREAM OF COCONUT (PREFERABLY COCO LOPEZ)

PINEAPPLE AND ORANGE SLICES, TO GARNISH

SERVES 10

Add all the ingredients to a blender with four scoops of crushed ice and blitz to mix. Pour into a jug/pitcher and serve in Tiki mugs (if you have them) garnished with fresh pineapple and orange slices.

Passionfruit Punch

★

If there's one thing Cuban music inspires, it's passion. Whether it's rumba, Afro-Cuban jazz, son cubano or salsa, each beat is sure to get your feet tapping and your hips swaying. The Passionfruit Punch will certainly inspire your thirst for rhythm… plus quench your dry mouth once you've built up a sweat.

300 ML/10 OZ. WHITE RUM

150 ML/5 OZ. PASSIONFRUIT PULP (FROM ABOUT 6 LARGE RIPE PASSIONFRUIT)

150 ML/5 OZ. FRESH ORANGE JUICE

600 ML/20 OZ. CLEAR SPARKLING LEMONADE

ICE CUBES, TO SERVE

SERVES 6

Put the rum, passionfruit pulp and orange juice in a large jug/pitcher and chill for an hour. Half-fill six tall glasses with ice, add the rum and fruit juice mixture and top up with lemonade. Serve immediately.

Caribbean Flip

★

A flip is a type of mixed drink dating back to 1695, although it's evolved a lot since then. The first bar guide to include a flip was Jerry Thomas's *How to Mix Drinks* back in 1862. This Caribbean version is rich, luxurious and warming – and is delicious with either dark rums, which will mean sugar and spice and all things nice, or lighter rums, which will bring out the orange of the Curaçao and the aromas from the bitters. Your taste buds will certainly flip with delight.

100 ML/3½ OZ. RUM

25 ML/1 OZ. ORANGE CURAÇAO

50 ML/1¾ OZ. DARK SUGAR SYRUP
(SEE PAGE 17)

75 ML/2½ OZ. DOUBLE/HEAVY CREAM

2 DASHES OF ANGOSTURA BITTERS

A PINCH OF GROUND CINNAMON

1 SMALL EGG YOLK

CINNAMON STICK AND FRESHLY GRATED
NUTMEG, TO GARNISH

Shake all the ingredients very hard with ice for at least 30 seconds; the harder you shake, the lighter the texture will be. Strain into a chilled wine glass and garnish with a long stick of cinnamon and some freshly grated nutmeg to serve.

Sailors in the 18th century were often paid in rum. To test its authenticity, they mixed it with gunpowder – if it ignited, it was the real deal.

Still Ginger Lemonade

The national flower of Cuba is the *Hedychium coronarium* – more commonly known as the 'white ginger lily'. It's often referred to as 'flor de mariposa', meaning 'butterfly flower', due to its similarity in shape to the creature. One sip of this zingy drink and your taste buds will flutter to cloud nine.

A 10-CM/4-INCH PIECE OF FRESH GINGER, PEELED AND VERY FINELY SLICED

FRESH JUICE OF 4 LEMONS

1 LEMON, SLICED

75 G/6 TABLESPOONS WHITE SUGAR

SERVES 4

Put the ginger, lemon juice, sliced lemon and sugar in a heatproof jug/pitcher and pour over 1 litre/quart boiling water. Mix well and let steep for 2 hours. Chill, then serve poured over crushed ice.

Top tip:

Many variations can be made of this drink. If you don't like lemons, use limes or oranges and, for a really clean taste, add mint. If you want something stronger, add a shot of rum to each glass.

Grown-Up Lemonade

Very similar to the Mojito – but replacing the lime for lemon – this luscious libation will renew your zest for life and laughter. Zing it on!

125 ML/4 OZ. FRESH LEMON JUICE

3 TABLESPOONS WHITE SUGAR

2 LEMONS, THINLY SLICED

A HANDFUL OF FRESH MINT LEAVES

125 ML/4 OZ. WHITE RUM

750 ML/¾ QUART SODA WATER

ICE CUBES, TO SERVE

SERVES 6

Combine the lemon juice and sugar in a small saucepan. Cook over high heat until boiling, then reduce the heat to medium and simmer for 4–5 minutes, until syrupy. Let cool.

Put the cooled lemon syrup with the ice cubes, lemon slices, mint and rum in a large jug/pitcher. Stir to combine and add the soda water. Serve immediately.

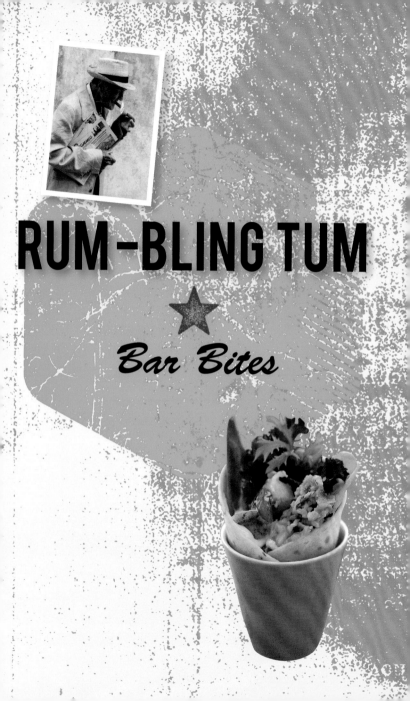

RUM-BLING TUM

★

Bar Bites

Spicy Mixed Nuts

Even though this recipe calls for cashews, pecans and pistachios, other nuts will work just as well. Peanuts – which grow in abundance in Cuba – would be particularly delicious. In Havana, peanut vendors are everywhere, tempting passers-by with roasted, salted and sugared kernels.

155 G/1¼ CUPS UNSALTED CASHEWS
155 G/1¼ CUPS PECANS
140 G/1 CUP PISTACHIOS
1 TEASPOON CAYENNE PEPPER
1 TEASPOON SMOKED PAPRIKA (PIMENTÓN)
½ TEASPOON DRIED THYME

1 TEASPOON FINE SEA SALT
1 TABLESPOON SOFT BROWN SUGAR
1 TABLESPOON OLIVE OIL

A BAKING SHEET, LINED
WITH BAKING PARCHMENT
SERVES 10–12

Preheat the oven to 180°C (350°F) Gas 4.

Put all the nuts in a large bowl. Add the cayenne pepper, paprika, thyme, sea salt and brown sugar, and mix to combine. Stir in the olive oil. Tip the nuts out onto the prepared baking sheet, spreading them out into a single layer.

Bake in the preheated oven for 10 minutes, stirring about halfway through the cooking time. Let cool completely before spooning into serving bowls. Perfect served with any of the drinks recipes in this book, these nuts will keep in an airtight container for 7–10 days.

Sweet Potato Fries

While there are more than 6,500 sweet potato varieties in the world, if you want to go for Cuban authenticity, use the boniato potato for these fries – more commonly known as the Cuban sweet potato. This recipe uses olive oil, but coconut oil can be used instead for a more tropical taste.

4 SWEET POTATOES, CUT TO DESIRED SIZE AND THICKNESS

2–3 TABLESPOONS OLIVE OIL

1 TABLESPOON SALT

1 TABLESPOON GROUND BLACK PEPPER

¼ TEASPOON CAYENNE PEPPER (OPTIONAL)

2 LARGE BAKING SHEETS, OILED

SERVES 4

Preheat the oven to 200°C (400°F) Gas 6.

In a resealable plastic bag, combine the sweet potatoes, olive oil, salt, black pepper and cayenne pepper. Close and shake the bag until the sweet potatoes are evenly coated. Spread them out in a single layer on the prepared baking sheets.

Bake in the preheated oven for 30 minutes, or until the sweet potatoes are crispy and brown on one side. Turn the fries over using a spatula, and cook for another 30 minutes, until they are all crispy on the outside and tender inside.

Guacamole

This creamy, addictive dip has been filling people's bellies since the 16th century, and its popularity shows no signs of wavering. On average, around 53 million pounds of the green stuff is consumed in the U.S. every Super Bowl Sunday. Team it with tortilla chips, salads, sandwiches or chicken wings. Touchdown!

6 AVOCADOS, PEELED, STONED/PITTED AND MASHED

FRESH JUICE OF 2 LIMES

2 TEASPOONS SALT

1 LARGE ONION, DICED

5 TABLESPOONS CHOPPED FRESH CORIANDER/CILANTRO

4 PLUM TOMATOES, DICED

2 TEASPOONS FINELY CHOPPED GARLIC

CAYENNE PEPPER, TO TASTE

In a large bowl, combine and mash together the avocados, lime juice and salt. When incorporated, mix in the onion, coriander/cilantro, tomatoes and garlic. Stir in cayenne pepper to taste and add more salt if needed. Refrigerate for 1 hour before serving for the best flavour.

Salsa

Opt for a spicy jalapeño pepper when preparing this salsa so that, like the Cuban-style dance, it'll be hot, intense and leave you wanting more…

3 LARGE TOMATOES, CHOPPED

1 GREEN (BELL) PEPPER, CHOPPED

1 RED ONION, DICED

20 G/¼ CUP FINELY CHOPPED FRESH CORIANDER/CILANTRO

2 TABLESPOONS FRESH LIME JUICE

½–1 JALAPEÑO PEPPER, FINELY CHOPPED

½ TEASPOON GROUND CUMIN

1 TEASPOON SEA SALT FLAKES

1 TEASPOON GROUND BLACK PEPPER

Combine all the ingredients in a bowl. Serve immediately or cover and refrigerate until required.

Salsa Verde

Turn up the heat with this piquant dip, which unites two of Cuba's most commonly used spices in cooking: cumin and garlic.

225-G/8-OZ. CAN OF TOMATILLOS, DRAINED, OR FRESH

½ SMALL ONION, CHOPPED

1 GARLIC CLOVE, FINELY CHOPPED

1 FRESH GREEN CHILLI/CHILE, FINELY CHOPPED

2 TABLESPOONS CHOPPED FRESH CORIANDER/CILANTRO

¼ TEASPOON GROUND CUMIN

1 TEASPOON SALT, OR TO TASTE

ALL DIPS SERVE 6–8

Combine all the ingredients in a saucepan with 250 ml/1 cup water. Bring to a boil over a high heat, then reduce the heat to medium–low and simmer for 10–15 minutes until the tomatillos are soft. Purée the mixture in a blender until smooth (you may need to do this in batches). Serve immediately or cover and refrigerate until required.

Papaya Ginger Salsa

If you serve this salsa to any Cuban guests, be aware that 'papaya' is a slang term for 'vagina', so you may want to rename it 'Fruta Bomba Ginger Salsa' to avoid any awkward titters at the dinner table.

1 RED (BELL) PEPPER

1 YELLOW (BELL) PEPPER

A 5-CM/2-INCH PIECE OF FRESH GINGER, PEELED AND GRATED

GRATED ZEST AND FRESH JUICE OF 2 LIMES, PLUS LIME WEDGES, TO SERVE

1 TEASPOON WHITE SUGAR, OR TO TASTE (OPTIONAL)

1 LARGE RED CHILLI/CHILE, DESEEDED AND CHOPPED

1 RIPE PAPAYA, PEELED, DESEEDED AND CUBED

A LARGE HANDFUL OF FRESH CORIANDER/CILANTRO LEAVES

SEA SALT AND GROUND BLACK PEPPER

SERVES 4

Peel the (bell) peppers with a vegetable peeler, then cut off the tops and bottoms, scoop out the seeds and membranes and cut the flesh down one side. Open each (bell) pepper out into a long rectangle. Cut the rectangle into 1-cm/½-inch squares.

Squeeze the grated ginger through a garlic press into a serving bowl. Add the lime juice and sugar, and salt and pepper to taste. Mix with a fork, then add the (bell) peppers and chilli/chile. Toss gently, then add the papaya, coriander/cilantro and lime zest and toss gently again so as not to break up the papaya. Top with the lime wedges and serve.

Salt Cod Peppers

The piquillo pepper is a variety of chilli/chile that tastes sweet instead of scorching. They are small, so perfect for tapas – pretend you're dining in Havana's cool tapas bar El Chanchullero, abuzz with the city's lively music, cool vibe and colourful characters. If you can't get hold of any piquillo peppers, substitute them for jarred roasted red (bell) peppers or chargrill some red (bell) peppers yourself, let cool and discard the blackened skins.

150 G/6 OZ. BONELESS SALT COD

200 ML/SCANT 1 CUP WHOLE MILK

1 SMALL ONION, FINELY SLICED

2 BAY LEAVES

A SPRIG OF FRESH FLAT-LEAF PARSLEY

25 G/2 TABLESPOONS UNSALTED BUTTER

2 TABLESPOONS PLAIN/ALL-PURPOSE FLOUR

8 CANNED PIQUILLO PEPPERS, DRAINED

SEA SALT AND GROUND WHITE PEPPER

SLICED BREAD, TO SERVE (OPTIONAL)

SERVES 4

To prepare the salt cod, soak it in cold water for 24 hours, changing the water every 4–5 hours. Just before you are ready to use it, drain well.

Put the milk in a saucepan, then add the onion, bay leaves and parsley, and set over a medium heat. Cook almost to boiling, then remove from the heat and let cool before straining. Melt the butter in a separate saucepan, then stir in the flour and cook over a medium heat for 1 minute. Slowly stir in the strained milk. Continue to cook for 3 minutes or until the mixture is thick. Season with salt and pepper and let cool.

Put the cod in a saucepan and cover with cold water. Bring to the boil, then simmer for 20 minutes. Remove and pat dry with paper towels. Remove the skin and flake the flesh into a bowl, making sure to remove all the bones. Pour in the white sauce and mix well. Stuff into the cavity of the peppers. Refrigerate for 2 hours or overnight.

Preheat the oven to 150°C (300°F) Gas 2.

Transfer the peppers to an ovenproof dish and cook in the preheated oven for 15 minutes before serving.

Camarones a la Plancha

Shrimp: the small crustacean with the big personality. Celebrate the fact that shrimp farming in Cuba has increased over recent years with this tasty dish. The simple accompanying salsa is full of flavour and accentuates, rather than overpowers, the shrimp. Pictured on page 102.

2 TOMATOES

1 TABLESPOON VERY FINELY CHOPPED ONION

1 GREEN CHILLI/CHILE

1 SMALL BUNCH OF CORIANDER/CILANTRO, FINELY CHOPPED

¼ TEASPOON SEA SALT

15 G/1½ TABLESPOONS BUTTER

6 LARGE PRAWNS/SHRIMP, SHELL ON

5 GARLIC CLOVES, VERY FINELY CHOPPED

SERVES 2

Put the tomatoes, onion, chilli/chile and 500 ml/2 cups water in a saucepan over high heat. Cover with a lid and bring to the boil, then turn the heat down to low and simmer for about 5–7 minutes.

Drain, then allow to cool for at least 5 minutes before transferring to a food processor with the coriander/cilantro and half the salt. Whizz for 2 minutes and set aside.

Preheat a stovetop grill pan or frying pan/skillet over medium heat.

Put the butter and prawns/shrimp in the pan and cook for 3–4 minutes or until opaque and cooked through, turning occasionally. Add the garlic and cook for 2 minutes.

Divide the prawns/shrimp between 2 dishes and spoon some of the coriander/cilantro sauce over them. Serve with the remaining sauce on the side for dipping.

Shellfish Cocktail Wraps with Guacamole

Lobster is a rarity in Cuba, reserved for tourists and export, and is often sold on the black market. At one particular spot on the Cuban coastline, just north of Valle Viñales, the lobsters are so abundant that they can be caught with your bare hands and a bucket. When shopping for the ingredients for this dish, be grateful that you're in a store or a fishmonger rather than wading in the surf and trying to avoid the police patrol on the lookout for lobster smugglers.

3 TABLESPOONS MAYONNAISE

A FEW DROPS OF TABASCO SAUCE

1 TEASPOON SUN-DRIED TOMATO PASTE

150–180 G/5½–6½ OZ. LOBSTER MEAT OR WILD CRAYFISH TAILS, FRESHLY COOKED

4 X 20-CM/8-INCH TORTILLA WRAPS

GUACAMOLE (SEE PAGE 106)

A SMALL HANDFUL OF BABY SALAD LEAVES WITH HERBS

LEMON WEDGES, TO SERVE

MAKES 8 AND SERVES 4

To make the shellfish cocktail, mix the mayonnaise, Tabasco and sun-dried tomato paste together in a bowl. If using lobster, chop the meat into bite-sized pieces. Add the lobster or crayfish tails to the bowl and mix together.

Lay the tortilla wraps out on a clean work surface and top each one with guacamole, baby salad leaves and shellfish cocktail. Roll each wrap tightly and cut in half. Serve with lemon wedges.

Chilli Salt Squid

With its ample coral reef, crystal-clear waters and vast array of marine life, Cuba has some of the best snorkelling and scuba-diving spots in the world. Schools of squid are plentiful and, once caught, make for some tasty tentacles.

400 G/14 OZ. CLEANED SQUID

2 TABLESPOONS CORNFLOUR/CORNSTARCH

1 TABLESPOON PLAIN/ALL-PURPOSE FLOUR

½ TEASPOON GROUND WHITE PEPPER

½ TEASPOON MILD CHILLI POWDER

3 TEASPOONS SEA SALT

1 LARGE RED CHILLI/CHILE, THINLY SLICED

A SMALL HANDFUL OF FRESH CORIANDER/CILANTRO LEAVES, CHOPPED

VEGETABLE OIL, FOR DEEP-FRYING

LEMON WEDGES, TO SERVE

SERVES 4

Cut the squid tube down one side so that it opens up. Use a sharp knife to trim and discard any internal membranes. Cut it lengthways into 2 cm/¾-inch wide strips, then cut each strip in half. Combine the cornflour/cornstarch, plain/all-purpose flour, white pepper, chilli powder and salt in a large bowl. Half-fill a saucepan with the vegetable oil and set over a high heat until the surface of the oil shimmers.

Toss half of the squid pieces in the flour mixture, quickly shaking off the excess, and add them to the hot oil. Cook for about 2 minutes, until deep golden in colour. Remove with a slotted spoon and drain on paper towels. Repeat with the remaining squid.

Add the chilli/chile slices to the oil and cook for just a few seconds. Remove from the pan and drain on paper towels. Put the squid and chilli/chile on a serving plate and sprinkle with the coriander/cilantro.

Serve while still warm with plenty of lemon wedges on the side.

Corn Flautas

Flautas are usually made with corn tortillas, but are equally appetizing with flour ones. Whichever you choose, fill and cook in the same way; both make the perfect appetizer to serve with drinks.

200 G/7 OZ. COOKED CHICKEN BREAST
FILLETS, CUT INTO STRIPS

80 G/½ CUP CUMBLED FETA CHEESE

2 TABLESPOONS CHOPPED FRESH
CORIANDER/CILANTRO

4 SPRING ONIONS/SCALLIONS, CHOPPED

1 SMALL RED CHILLI/CHILE, DESEEDED
AND FINELY CHOPPED

8 X 15-CM/6-INCH TORTILLA WRAPS

SUNFLOWER OIL, FOR FRYING

SOUR CREAM AND SALSA (SEE PAGE 106),
TO SERVE

MAKES 16 AND SERVES 4–6

Preheat the oven to 150°C (300°F) Gas 2.

In a bowl, mix together the chicken, feta cheese, coriander/cilantro, spring onions/scallions and chilli/chile. Warm the tortilla wraps by covering in foil and put in the oven, to soften, or wrap in clingfilm/plastic wrap and heat for about 30–45 seconds in a microwave.

Put a spoonful of chicken filling on one edge of each tortilla and roll up into flutes, tucking the ends in. Secure with a toothpick. Cover with clingfilm/plastic wrap until ready to cook, to prevent them drying out.

Preheat a heavy-based non-stick frying pan/skillet filled with oil to a depth of about 2.5 cm/1 inch, until the oil is hot. Add half the flautas and fry for about 3 minutes, until crisp and golden, turning frequently. Drain on paper towels and keep hot while cooking the remaining flautas.

Remove the toothpicks, cut each flauta in half diagonally and serve with the sour cream and salsa.

Chicken Mole Burrito

'Burrito' means 'little donkey' in Spanish. As you tuck into this dinner, spare a thought for Cuba's famous 'donkey of Bainoa', said to have roamed the streets of this small town being offered beer by locals. The crazy ass often became intoxicated and was the source of much amusement due to his drunken silliness.

500 G/1 LB. 2 OZ. BONELESS SKINLESS CHICKEN

CHICKEN OR VEGETABLE STOCK, OR WATER, AS REQUIRED

1 TABLESPOON VEGETABLE OIL

1 LARGE ONION, FINELY CHOPPED

200 G/1 CUP GOOD-QUALITY MOLE POBLANO PASTE

300 G/1½ CUPS COOKED RICE

400 G/14 OZ. CANNED PINTO BEANS, DRAINED

4–6 LARGE TORTILLA WRAPS

180 G/SCANT 2 CUPS GRATED CHEDDAR OR MONTEREY JACK CHEESE

SEA SALT AND GROUND BLACK PEPPER, TO TASTE

A BAKING SHEET OR SHALLOW OVENPROOF DISH, OILED

SERVES 4–6

Preheat the oven to 150°C (300°F) Gas 2.

Put the chicken in a large saucepan and add enough stock or water to cover. If using water or unseasoned stock, season with salt.

Bring to the boil over medium heat, then cover and simmer gently for 30–40 minutes until cooked through and tender. Remove the chicken from the pan and let cool slightly, then shred using your hands or two forks. Taste and adjust the seasoning.

Heat the oil in a saucepan set over medium–high heat. Add the onion and cook for about 5–8 minutes, stirring occasionally, until golden. Stir in the mole paste and dilute according to the packet instructions, using a little stock or water. Cook for 1–2 minutes further. Add the shredded chicken, rice and beans and mix well. Simmer over low heat for 10–15 minutes.

Divide the chicken mixture between the tortillas and sprinkle with grated cheese. Fold in the sides of each tortilla to cover the filling, then roll up to enclose. Put the filled tortillas seam-side down on the prepared baking sheet or shallow dish. Cover with foil and bake in the preheated oven for 10–15 minutes just to warm through and melt the cheese. Serve hot.

Chilli con Carne Empañadillas

Many countries – from Argentina to Brazil, Singapore to Mexico – have made their own stamp on the empañada, varying the dough, fillings and seasonings. Cuban empañadas are typically filled with beef or chicken, but can also be made with cheese. Sweet varieties contain apples, pears, pumpkins and pineapples. The amount of pastry here allows for 60 empañadillas (mini empañadas). Halve the recipe if you are only cooking for a small number or freeze any extra pastry.

4 TABLESPOONS OLIVE OIL

400 G/14 OZ. MINCED/GROUND BEEF

2 ONIONS, DICED

4 GARLIC CLOVES

600 ML/2¹⁄₂ CUPS BEEF STOCK

400 G/14 OZ. CANNED CHOPPED TOMATOES

4 TABLESPOONS TOMATO PURÉE/PASTE

¹⁄₂ TEASPOON CHIPOTLE PASTE

1 TEASPOON CHILLI/HOT RED PEPPER FLAKES

1 TEASPOON COCOA POWDER

80 G/¹⁄₂ CUP COOKED RED KIDNEY BEANS

SEA SALT AND GROUND BLACK PEPPER, TO TASTE

PASTRY

250 G/2 STICKS PLUS 2 TABLESPOONS BUTTER, CHILLED AND CUBED

450 G/3³⁄₄ CUPS PLAIN/ALL-PURPOSE FLOUR

1 EGG

60 ML/¹⁄₄ CUP COLD WATER

¹⁄₂ TEASPOON SALT

1 EGG, BEATEN

A 7.5-CM/3-INCH COOKIE CUTTER

MAKES 60

First, prepare the pastry. Put all of the ingredients except the beaten egg into the food processor and blitz until a dough forms. Add a little more water if the dough doesn't come together. Wrap the dough in clingfilm/plastic wrap and refrigerate for at least 30 minutes.

To make the filling, preheat 2 tablespoons of the oil in a large frying pan/skillet set over a medium heat and brown the minced/ground beef. Transfer the meat to a large mixing bowl and, in the same pan, fry the onions and garlic in the remaining oil until softened. Return the meat to the pan and pour over the stock, canned tomatoes, tomato puree/paste, chipotle paste and chilli/hot red pepper flakes, and cook for 40 minutes. Add the cocoa powder and the kidney beans and warm through. Season to taste then cool completely. For best results, refrigerate for 24 hours.

Preheat the oven to 200°C (400°F) Gas 6.

Roll out the dough to 3-mm/⅛-inch thick. Use the cutter to stamp out discs. Lay the discs out on a lightly floured surface and put a heaped teaspoon of filling in the middle. Moisten the top half of the dough with a little water. Pull over the other half of dough, taking care to squeeze out any air. You can do this by pressing down on the edge of the dough with the tines of a fork or by folding and pinching the edges over. Arrange on a baking sheet, brush with a little of the beaten egg and bake in the preheated oven for 15–20 minutes, or until golden. Serve hot.

Pineapple-Habañero Wings

Named after the Cuban city of La Habana (Havana) as it is thought to have originated there, the habañero pepper is hotter than a pistol! So hot, in fact, that it's rated between 100,000 and 350,000 on the Scoville scale. In comparison, the bell pepper is rated 0.

125 G/½ CUP CRUSHED PINEAPPLE

120 ML/½ CUP SOUR CREAM

2 TABLESPOONS HABAÑERO SAUCE
OR OTHER HOT SAUCE

¼ TEASPOON SALT

VEGETABLE OIL, FOR FRYING

1.8 KG/4 LBS. CHICKEN WINGS, HALVED
AT THE JOINTS, TIPS REMOVED

70 G/½ CUP PLAIN/ALL-PURPOSE FLOUR

PINEAPPLE DIPPING SAUCE

225 G/1 CUP PLAIN YOGURT

125 G/½ CUP CRUSHED PINEAPPLE

2 TABLESPOONS ICING/CONFECTIONERS'
SUGAR

25 G/¼ CUP SHREDDED/DESSICATED
COCONUT

2 TABLESPOONS COCONUT MILK

SERVES 4–6

Combine the crushed pineapple, sour cream, habañero sauce or other hot sauce and salt in a medium saucepan; whisk until smooth. Set over a low–medium heat and warm through.

To make the pineapple dipping sauce, combine all the ingredients in a serving bowl and refrigerate until ready to serve.

Preheat the oil in a deep fryer set to 180°C (350°F).

Coat the chicken wings with flour by dredging them or tossing them in a bowl. Fry a few wings at a time for 10 minutes or until golden and crispy and the juices run clear when the thickest part is pierced to the bone. Toss the wings with warm pineapple-habañero sauce and serve with the pineapple dipping sauce.

Jerk Chicken

'Jerk' is a style of cooking involving seasoning and grilling meats in a spicy deliciousness originally hailing from the Caribbean island of Jamaica. It's time to get marinating, people!

1 TABLESPOON GROUND ALLSPICE

1 TEASPOON DRIED THYME

1½ TEASPOONS CAYENNE PEPPER

1½ TEASPOONS GROUND BLACK PEPPER

1½ TEASPOONS DRIED SAGE

¾ TEASPOON GROUND NUTMEG

¾ TEASPOON GROUND CINNAMON

1 TABLESPOON WHITE SUGAR

4 TABLESPOONS OLIVE OIL

4 TABLESPOONS SOY SAUCE

175 ML/¾ CUP WHITE VINEGAR

125 ML/½ CUP ORANGE JUICE

FRESH JUICE OF 1 LIME

1 HABAÑERO OR SCOTCH BONNET CHILLI/CHILE, DESEEDED AND FINELY CHOPPED

3 SPRING ONIONS/SCALLIONS, FINELY CHOPPED

120 G/1 CUP ONION, FINELY CHOPPED

10 GARLIC CLOVES, CRUSHED

4–6 CHICKEN BREASTS, OR A WHOLE CHICKEN CUT INTO PIECES (SKIN LEFT ON)

SERVES 4

Combine the first 8 ingredients in a large bowl.

Combine the olive oil, soy sauce, vinegar, orange juice and lime juice in a large measuring cup or small bowl. Slowly add the spice mixture, whisking it in until incorporated. Add the habañero or Scotch bonnet chilli/chile, spring onions/scallions, onions and garlic and stir in.

Spread the marinade all over the chicken. Put in a large resealable plastic bag and seal tightly. Refrigerate overnight, or for at least 4 hours.

When ready to cook, heat up either a barbecue or a charcoal grill. Grill the chicken for about 6 minutes per side, brushing on more of the marinade while cooking and making sure that the marinade is well cooked as it will have been in contact with raw chicken for several hours. Test if the chicken is cooked by sticking a skewer in the thickest part – if the juices run clear, it is ready.

Bring the leftover marinade to a fast boil for at least 4 minutes and serve as a dipping sauce.

Cuban Rice

This Cuban-inspired rice dish, traditionally served at breakfast, is mostly eaten in Spanish-speaking countries. People can't seem to agree where this comfort food originated, but many believe it hails from Cuba when it was a Spanish colony. Don't let the unusual flavours of bacon, egg, tomato and a banana put you off: somehow they work.

4 TABLESPOONS OF SUNFLOWER OIL, PLUS EXTRA FOR FRYING

1 ONION, CHOPPED

2 GARLIC CLOVES, FINELY CHOPPED

4 TOMATOES, FINELY CHOPPED

1 TEASPOON WHITE WINE VINEGAR

1 TEASPOON DRIED OREGANO

2 RASHERS/STRIPS BACON, CHOPPED

250 G/GENEROUS 1¼ CUPS BOMBA, CALASPARRA OR ARBORIO RICE

600 ML/2½ CUPS HOT CHICKEN STOCK

2 BANANAS, HALVED

4 TABLESPOONS SEASONED FLOUR

4 EGGS

1 TABLESPOON CHOPPED FRESH CORIANDER/CILANTRO

SEA SALT AND GROUND BLACK PEPPER

A FEW ROCKET/ARUGULA LEAVES, TO SERVE

SERVES 4

Heat half the oil in a saucepan set over a low heat and fry the onions and garlic for 20 minutes, until caramelized, adding a little water if necessary to stop the onion burning. Stir in the tomatoes and simmer for a further 20 minutes, until the sauce is thick. Stir in the vinegar and oregano, and season to taste. Keep warm.

Heat the remaining oil in a frying pan/skillet set over a medium heat and fry the bacon for 3–4 minutes, until golden. Stir in the rice and then add the stock. Bring to the boil and simmer gently for 20 minutes, until al dente. Keep warm.

Dust the bananas with seasoned flour and shallow fry in sunflower oil for 1–2 minutes on each side, until golden. Remove with a slotted spoon, then fry the eggs until cooked to your liking.

Arrange the rice on serving plates and top each serving with a fried egg and half a banana. Sprinkle with coriander/cilantro and serve immediately with the tomato sauce and a little rocket/arugula.

Peppered Pineapple, Coconut and Rum Shots

Pineapple is plentiful in Cuba. In 2015, the country exported 700 tonnes of the thirst-quenching fruit to Europe. Chill the ingredients before you make these fun shots, then they're ready to serve straightaway. Alternatively, you can freeze the mixture, crush it and serve it as a granita.

300 G/10½ OZ. VERY RIPE PREPARED FRESH
PINEAPPLE FLESH
200 ML/¾ CUP COCONUT CREAM
100 ML/⅓ CUP WHITE RUM
2 TABLESPOONS MUSCOVADO SUGAR
¼ TEASPOON SEA SALT

TO SERVE
GRATED FRESH NUTMEG
GROUND BLACK PEPPER
CAYENNE PEPPER
SERVES 10–15

Put the pineapple, coconut cream, rum, sugar and salt in a blender or food processor and whizz until smooth and creamy. Transfer the mixture to a jug/pitcher and carefully pour into small shot glasses.

To finish, you can either grate over a little nutmeg, add a few grinds of black pepper or a sprinkling of cayenne pepper, as preferred.

Piña Colada Jellies

Crank up the volume as you dance around to Rupert Holmes' fun number-one 1979 hit 'Escape (The Piña Colada Song)', pausing for mouthfuls of this boozy jelly.

690 ML/SCANT 3 CUPS PINEAPPLE JUICE (NOT FROM CONCENTRATE)

34 SHEETS OF GELATINE, SOFTENED IN COLD WATER FOR 5–10 MINUTES

345 ML/1½ CUPS CHERRY JUICE

400 G /14 OZ. SWEETENED CONDENSED MILK

300 ML/1¼ CUPS MALIBU OR OTHER COCONUT-FLAVOURED WHITE RUM

80 ML/⅓ CUP COCONUT CREAM

A 25 X 18-CM/10 X 7-INCH AND A 12 X 9-CM/4½ X 3½-INCH CONTAINER, LINED WITH CLINGFILM/PLASTIC WRAP MAKES ABOUT 120 CUBES

Heat 120 ml/½ cup of the pineapple juice to a simmer in a saucepan. Take off the heat, squeeze the water out of 11 sheets of gelatine, add to the juice and whisk. Add this to the remaining pineapple juice and whisk. Pour into the larger prepared container and set in the refrigerator for at least 3 hours.

Heat 60 ml/¼ cup of the cherry juice to a simmer in a saucepan. Take off the heat, squeeze the water out of 6 sheets of gelatine, add to the juice and whisk. Add this to the remaining cherry juice and whisk. Pour into the smaller prepared container and set in the refrigerator for at least 3 hours.

Once both jellies are set, heat 180 ml/¾ cup water to a simmer in a saucepan. Take off the heat. Squeeze the water out of 17 sheets of gelatine, add to the water and whisk. Add this to the condensed milk, along with the Malibu, 150 ml/generous ½ cup of water and the coconut cream. Mix, then let cool but not set.

Cut the pineapple and cherry jellies into 1.5-cm/¾-inch cubes. Arrange the cubes in a container large enough to hold them all, then cover with the cooled coconut jelly to a depth of 2.5 cm/1 inch. Set in the refrigerator overnight.

The next day, cut into 2.5-cm/1-inch cubes to serve.

Index

Picture Credits

Peter Cassidy 102a, 105, 108,
120; Helen Cathcart 117, 125;
Jean Cazals 124; Addie Chinn
6, 20, 62a, 64; Richard Jung
87; Gavin Kingcome 2, 14-16,
18a, 36, 39, 46a, 60, 67, 81,
82; William Lingwood 11, 21,
24, 27, 33, 40, 48, 51, 55, 59,
71- 75, 84a, 86, 88-96, 101,
103b, 111, 114; Gareth
Morgans 28, 52; Martin Norris
1, 5, 19b, 22, 23, 30, 31, 35,
42 left, 43- 45, 47b, 63b, 68,
76- 79, 85b, 99, 128; Toby
Scott 107, 119; Ian Wallace
123; Kate Whitaker 56, 104,
113; 18b Emily Riddell/Getty
Images; 19a Anna Yu/Getty
Images; 38 cbaud/Getty Images
41 insert Anna Yu/Getty Images;
42 right Photos By Steve
Horsley/Getty Images; 46b
ilbusc/istock; 47a VanWyck
Express/istock; 58 flexx/istock;
61 altrendo images/Getty
Images; 62b VINMAG; 63a Anna
Yu/Getty Images; 84b Michal
Krakowiak/istock; 85a Byron
Motley/istock; 102b Brent
Winebrenner/Getty Images; 103a
Jeremy Woodhouse/Getty Images
Front jacket: left VINMAG; Centre
ilbusca/istock; right ph Addie
Chinn; left stamp raciro/istock;
right stamp;
AlexanderZam/istock
Back jacket: ph Addie Chinn
Endpapers: above
ArtMarie/istock; below left ph
Gavin Kingcome; below centre
Anna Yu/Getty Images; below
right altrendo images/Getty
Images.

Recipe Credits

MICHAEL BUTT
Ambrosia
Añejo Highball
Bazooka Joe
Caribbean Flip
Cubanada
Dry Daiquiri
June Bug
Mai Tai
Paradise Punch
Ron Collins
Rum Sombrero
Shelter from the
 Storm
Strawberry Daiquiri
Surfer on Acid

ROSS DOBSON
Chilli Salt Squid
Grown-up Lemonade
Spicy Mixed Nuts

LYDIA FRANCE
Peppered Pineapple,
 Coconut and Rum
 Shots
Papaya Ginger Salsa

**FELIPE FUENTES CRUZ
 AND BEN FORDHAM**
Camarones a la
 Plancha

CAROL HILKER
Guacamole, Salsa and
 Salsa Verde
Jerk Chicken
Pineapple-Haberñero
 Wings
Sweet Potato Fries

LOUISE PICKFORD
Cuban Rice
Passionfruit Punch

BEN REED
Air Mail
Bacardi Cocktail
Bay Breeze
Blanco Sangria
Chi Chi
Colonel Beach's
 Plantation Punch
Commodore Cocktail
Cuba Libre
Cuban Sangria
Dark and Stormy
Frozen Kiwi Daiquiri
Hemingway Daiquiri
Homemade Cola
 Cordial
Honey Colada
Jalisco Siesta
Kingston Cooler
The Knickerbocker
Mojito
Orange Daiquiri
Original Daiquiri
Piña Colada
Planter's Punch
Queen's Park Swizzle
Rum Runner
Tropical Punch

JENNIE SHAPTER
Corn Flautas with
 Tomato Salsa
Shellfish Cocktail
 Wraps with
 Guacamole

MILLI TAYLOR
Chilli con Carne
 Empañadillas
Piña Colada Jellies

SUNIL VIJAYAKAR
Iced Pina Colada

FRAN WARDE
Still Ginger Lemonade

LAURA WASHBURN
Chicken Mole Burrito
Peppers Stuffed with
 Salt Cod

WILLIAM YEOWARD
Malacón
Mulata Daisy
Officer's Nightcap
Penzance
Raspberry and Rose
 Mojito
Swizzle